Creatures Great and Small

Shari Last

Rabbits burrow underground.

Dogs just love to play around.

Pigs go oink and ducks go quack.

Squirrels chase a nutty snack.

Raccoons scavenge for their food.

By day, butterflies drink nectar sweet.

Porcupine spines will make you yell.

One spray from a skunk will make you smell.

The hooded cobra's poised to bite,

But crocodiles are ready for a fight.

A nest of silk the spider weaves.

Koalas eat poisonous leaves.

Penguins leap and dive for fish.

While Polar bears hunt for their next dish.

Sea turtles lay their eggs nearby.

Tigers creep, and pounce, and growl.

In their packs, the grey wolves howl.

Macaw, majestic on its perch.

Peregrine falcon - fastest on Earth.

Lions hunt prey with their pride.

Chameleons change colour to hide.

Pandas munch on bamboo leaves.

Sloths relax up in the trees.

Creatures great and creatures small . . .
Which are your favourite creatures of all?

First published in Great Britain in 2024
by **TELL ME MORE Books**

Text copyright ©2024 Shari Last
Design copyright ©2024 Shari Last

ISBN: 978-1-917200-07-3

Picture credits: Thanks to baddesigner.

All rights reserved. Without limiting the rights under the copyright reserved above, no part of this publication may be reproduced, stored in, or introduced into a retrieval system, or transmitted, in any form, or by any means (electronic, mechanical, photocopying, recording or otherwise), without the prior written permission of the copyright owner.

WWW.TELLMEMOREBOOKS.COM

www.ingramcontent.com/pod-product-compliance
Lightning Source LLC
Chambersburg PA
CBHW050749110526
44591CB00002B/24